Memories for My

This book is dedicated to:
_____
_____

Love always, from:
_____
_____

Copyright © 2011 Robert J. Pemberton

All Rights Reserved.

Also by Robert J. Pemberton

My Website Password Organizer
My Address Book
My Home Inventory Organizer
My To Do List
All About Me
My Friendship Book

View the full book list at:
www.arlington.com.au

Contents

IMPORTANT DATES	4
MY MOST CHERISHED MEMORIES	5
MY FAVORITE PEOPLE	7
MY FAVORITE BOOKS	8
MY FAVORITE AUTHORS	9
MY FAVORITE FOODS	10
MY FAVORITE RECIPES	11
MY FAVORITE RESTAURANTS	12
MY FAVORITE DRINKS	13
MY FAVORITE SPORTS	14
MY FAVORITE SPORTSMEN/SPORTSWOMEN	15
MY FAVORITE TV SHOWS	16
MY FAVORITE TV ACTORS/ACTRESSES	17
MY FAVORITE CARTOONS/COMICS	18
MY FAVORITE MOVIES	19
MY FAVORITE MOVIE STARS	20
MY FAVORITE MOVIE DIRECTORS	21
MY FAVORITE BANDS/SINGERS	22
MY FAVORITE PLAYS	23
MY FAVORITE SONGS	24
MY FAVORITE COMPOSERS	25
MY FAVORITE SAYINGS/QUOTES	26
MY FAVORITE POETS/POEMS	27
MY FAVORITE COLORS	28
MY FAVORITE NAMES	29
AT SCHOOL/COLLEGE/UNIVERSITY	30
AT WORK	31
MY HOBBIES/PASS TIMES	32
SOME WORDS OF WISDOM	33
PLACES I'VE LIVED	34
PLACES I'VE VISITED	35
PLACES I WANT TO VISIT	36
SOME THINGS I WISH I HAD DONE	37
THINGS I LIKE THE MOST	38
THINGS I LIKE THE LEAST	39
SUCCESSES	40
REGRETS	41
LANGUAGES	42
MY FAVORITE WEB SITES	43

PETS I HAVE HAD	44
MY FAVORITE ANIMALS/BIRDS	45
MY FAVORITE PLANTS/FLOWERS	46
THINGS THAT MAKE ME SMILE	47
HAPPINESS IS	48
MY FAVORITE CLOTHES	49
MY FAVORITE SHOES	50
MY FAVORITE GAMES	51
MY FAVORITE TOYS	52
MY FAVORITE CARS/MOTORBIKES	53
MY FAVORITE ARTISTS	54
MY FAVORITE INVENTIONS	55
MY FAVORITE DIETS THAT WORK	56
MY FAVORITE EXERCISES	57
MY HEALTH AND BEAUTY TIPS	58
MY FAVORITE GIFTS	59
ALWAYS REMEMBER	60
THE MOST IMPORTANT THINGS IN LIFE	61
SPIRITUAL BELIEFS	62
MY FAVORITE CHARITY ORGANIZATIONS	63
LITTLE THINGS TO BE THANKFUL FOR	64
MY OWN SEVEN WONDERS	65
FINAL WORDS	66
NOTES	67

IMPORTANT DATES

When and where I was born:

When and where I got married:

MY MOST CHERISHED MEMORIES

Some cherished memories I can share with you are:

MY MOST CHERISHED MEMORIES (Continued)

MY FAVORITE PEOPLE

My all time list of favorite people, or people I admire are:

MY FAVORITE BOOKS

My favorite books are/were:

MY FAVORITE AUTHORS

My favorite authors are:

MY FAVORITE FOODS

My favorite foods are:

MY FAVORITE RECIPES

My all time favorite recipes are:

MY FAVORITE RESTAURANTS

My all time favorite restaurants are:

MY FAVORITE DRINKS

My all time favorite drinks are:

MY FAVORITE SPORTS

My favorite sports are:

MY FAVORITE SPORTSMEN/SPORTSWOMEN

My favorite sportsmen are:

My favorite sportswomen are:

MY FAVORITE TV SHOWS

My favorite TV shows are/were:

MY FAVORITE TV ACTORS/ACTRESSES

My favorite TV actors are/were:

My favorite TV actresses are/were:

MY FAVORITE CARTOONS/COMICS

My favorite cartoons are/were:

My favorite comics are/were:

MY FAVORITE MOVIES

My favorite movies are/were:

MY FAVORITE MOVIE STARS

My favorite movie stars are:

MY FAVORITE MOVIE DIRECTORS

My favorite movie directors are:

MY FAVORITE BANDS/SINGERS

My favorite bands/singers are:

MY FAVORITE PLAYS

My favorite plays are:

MY FAVORITE SONGS

My favorite songs are:

MY FAVORITE COMPOSERS

My favorite composers are:

MY FAVORITE SAYINGS/QUOTES

My favorite sayings, quotes or proverbs are:

MY FAVORITE POETS/POEMS

My favorite poets and poems are:

MY FAVORITE COLORS

My favorite colors are:

MY FAVORITE NAMES

My favorite boys names are:

My favorite girls names are:

AT SCHOOL/COLLEGE/UNIVERSITY

My favorite subjects were:

My worst subjects were:

I went to school at:

My highest level of education was:

AT WORK

My first job was:

I've had these jobs:

My favorite job was:

MY HOBBIES/PASS TIMES

My favorite hobbies/pass times are:

SOME WORDS OF WISDOM

Some words of wisdom for you:

PLACES I'VE LIVED

I've lived at these places:

PLACES I'VE VISITED

These are some of the best places I've visited:

PLACES I WANT TO VISIT

These are some of the places I want(ed) to visit

SOME THINGS I WISH I HAD DONE

I always wish I had done the following things:

THINGS I LIKE THE MOST

The things I like most are:

THINGS I LIKE THE LEAST

Things I like the least are:

SUCCESSES

I consider these to be my greatest successes:

REGRETS

These are some regrets I can share with you:

LANGUAGES

I can speak these languages:

I always wished I could speak these languages:

MY FAVORITE WEB SITES

These are my favorite websites:

PETS I HAVE HAD

These are the pets I've had over the years:

MY FAVORITE ANIMALS/BIRDS

This is a list of my favorite animals and birds:

MY FAVORITE PLANTS/FLOWERS

My favorite plants and flowers are:

THINGS THAT MAKE ME SMILE

These are some of the things that make me smile:

HAPPINESS IS

My definition of happiness is:

MY FAVORITE CLOTHES

My favorite clothes are/were:

MY FAVORITE SHOES

My favorite shoes are:

MY FAVORITE GAMES

My favorite games are:

MY FAVORITE TOYS

My all time favorite toys were/are:

MY FAVORITE CARS/MOTORBIKES

My all time favorite cars/motorbikes were/are:

MY FAVORITE ARTISTS

My favorite artists are:

MY FAVORITE INVENTIONS

My favorite inventions of all time are:

MY FAVORITE DIETS THAT WORK

My favorite diets that work are:

MY FAVORITE EXERCISES

My favorite exercises for keeping fit are:

MY HEALTH AND BEAUTY TIPS

My tips for good health are:

My tips for looking good are:

MY FAVORITE GIFTS

My favorite gifts for receiving are:

My favorite gifts for giving are:

ALWAYS REMEMBER

As you go through life, always remember:

THE MOST IMPORTANT THINGS IN LIFE

The most important things in life are:

SPIRITUAL BELIEFS

I would like to share the following spiritual beliefs with you:

MY FAVORITE CHARITY ORGANIZATIONS

My favorite charity organizations are:

LITTLE THINGS TO BE THANKFUL FOR

Some little things I believe we should be thankful for:

MY OWN SEVEN WONDERS

If I could choose the seven wonders they would be:

FINAL WORDS

NOTES

NOTES